THE
ROMANTIC CHILD

THIS IS THE TWENTIETH OF THE
WALTER NEURATH MEMORIAL LECTURES
WHICH ARE GIVEN ANNUALLY EACH SPRING ON
SUBJECTS REFLECTING THE INTERESTS OF
THE FOUNDER
OF THAMES AND HUDSON

THE DIRECTORS WISH TO EXPRESS
PARTICULAR GRATITUDE TO THE GOVERNORS AND
MASTER OF BIRKBECK COLLEGE
UNIVERSITY OF LONDON
FOR THEIR GRACIOUS SPONSORSHIP OF
THESE LECTURES

THE
ROMANTIC CHILD
FROM RUNGE TO
SENDAK

ROBERT ROSENBLUM

THAMES AND HUDSON

To Sophie and Theodore, post-Romantic children

First published in the United States in 1989 by
Thames and Hudson Inc., 500 Fifth Avenue,
New York, New York 10110

Library of Congress Catalog Card Number 88–50253

Printed and bound in Great Britain

Unlike most of my nineteen predecessors in this distinguished series, I never had the privilege of meeting the man to whom it pays tribute. But at least I know Walter Neurath in the best of indirect ways, through his family and through his publishing house. For me, in fact, the Neuraths—Eva, Thomas, and Constance—offer the happiest combination of personal and professional pleasure: people who are good friends and who also, it turns out, publish books that I write and books that I want to read. I hope the publication of this lecture sustains this wonderful tradition.

As for the lecture itself, delivered on March 28, 1988, I should explain that it was not read verbatim from a manuscript, but given more informally as commentary on over sixty slides. As a result, adaptations have had to be made for the printed version, including a reduction of illustrations and, I hope, a tightening of language more suitable for reading than for listening. I should say, too, that this lecture was a distillation of an interest I have long had not only in Runge but in the depiction of children in the Romantic period; and that on May 3, 1981, on the occasion of a symposium on German nineteenth-century painting held at the Metropolitan Museum of Art, New York, I first explored, in much briefer and more tentative form, some of the ideas expanded here. Moreover, I have written before about some of the paintings and comparisons included here, most conspicuously in my Modern Painting and the Northern Romantic Tradition; Friedrich to Rothko, *which Thames and Hudson published in 1975. For me, then, this lecture is both an end and a beginning: a condensation of earlier thoughts I have had about this topic, and a suggestion of what, I realize, might easily be expanded into a book-length international study.*

The topic, it turns out, is now most topical; and I discovered, after delivering the lecture, that the most important Runge scholar, Jörg Traeger, had only last year published a brief essay on a similar theme: Philipp Otto Runge; Die Hülsenbeckschen Kinder; Von der Reflexion des Naiven im Kunstwerk der Romantik, *Frankfurt am Main, 1987. Uncomfortable as I frankly was to see at this last moment many of my own ideas and illustrations offered in Traeger's excellent study, I also felt comforted by the fact that the subject was now so ripe, and Runge's innovations so potent, that art historians on both sides of the Atlantic would tackle the same questions and converge in their approaches.*

ROBERT ROSENBLUM
New York, May 1988

1 Runge, detail of
The Hülsenbeck Children,
1805–06

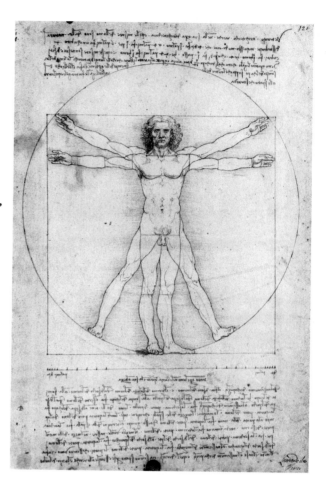

2 Leonardo da Vinci,
Vitruvian Man, c.1490

3 Runge, *The Child*,
1809

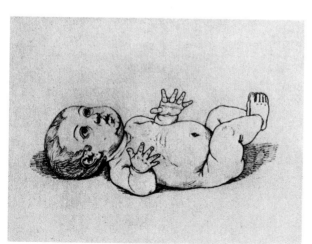

MUCH AS LEONARDO DA VINCI'S drawing of a nude inscribed in a 2
perfect square and circle has come to symbolize the concept of
"Renaissance Man," so, too, might a small lost drawing by the hero of 3
this lecture, Philipp Otto Runge, be invoked as a symbol of what might
be called "The Romantic Child."[1] At first, it may appear simply to be
an intensely observed record of the pudgy flesh, upward stare, and
reaching grasp of an infant lying helplessly on its back with the soles of
its feet pressed together as if in prayer. But in the context of Runge's art
and writings, this drawing of 1809 can also be seen to evoke a state of
natural innocence and religious purity so primal that the vision of a
sacred beginning to a radiantly new and magical world can hover in our
imagination above the baby's fixed gaze.

Before pursuing such mystical generalizations, however, a background to Runge's achievement must quickly be sketched in. As recent
studies of family life by such historians as Philippe Ariès or Lawrence
Stone have been demonstrating,[2] attitudes towards children and their
upbringing changed drastically from the mid-eighteenth century on.
Among the most obvious reversals of tradition among the upper classes
was the new enthusiasm for breastfeeding, a return to a natural, simple
maternal bond propagated, above all, by Jean-Jacques Rousseau, who,
in works of the 1760s like *Julie* (1761) and *Emile* (1762), challenged the
conventions of maternal indifference to children who would custom-
arily have been sent off to wet nurses and boarding schools, where the
psychological damage must often have been acute and the shocking
mortality rates more objectively measurable.[3] The responses to
Rousseau's advocacy of a mother's nursing her own children and of
tender, parental affection can be easily demonstrated in many paintings

4 Greuze, *La Mère Bien-Aimée*, c.1769

from both sides of the Channel. For instance, in Jean-Baptiste Greuze's
4 *La Mère Bien-Aimée*,[4] prepared for the Salon of 1769, the point could
hardly be more emphatic. For here, the Marquis de Laborde, the
wealthy financier who commissioned the painting, has had himself
depicted as just returning home from the hunt, extending his loving
arms to greet his doting mother-in-law and his blessed wife, who appears
to be ecstatically happy at the altar of maternity, her breasts and heart
easily available to all six of their worshipful children. Some five years
later, in 1774, Sir Joshua Reynolds exhibited at the Royal Academy a
comparably secular translation of a Christian exemplar of maternity and
5 charity, in this case again an aristocrat, Lady Cockburn of Eyemouth,
whose three sons, William, James, and George, move in child
development from a totally naked, breastfeeding infant to puckishly
adorable, nearly naked angels happily embraced by their mother.

10

5 Reynolds, *Lady Cockburn and her Children*, 1773

6 Graff, *The Artist's Family*, 1785

A part from the introduction of nursing mothers and children in the domain of family portraits of the later eighteenth century, the whole tenor of relations between children and parents began to change in the direction of a growingly casual and closely-knit domesticity. In the case, for instance, of artists who painted themselves in the context of their own families, the children, rather than appearing to be acting out in costume and demeanor the role of adults, begin to behave naturally or, perhaps better said, childishly. It is a point borne out, for one, in a family portrait 6 of 1785 by the Swiss-born Anton Graff, who would later befriend Runge during the younger artist's visit to Dresden in 1801. In this painting,[5] Graff's wife and children seem totally and easily integrated into the artist's private and professional family life. Ranging in age from four to eleven, Graff's daughter and two sons assume postures of domestic intimacy, study, and relaxation, preoccupied with reading, looking at pictures or simply kneeling on the floor smiling, in an attitude of childish reverie. Indeed, more and more, as 1800 approaches, these intimate glimpses of the realities of child behaviour can even introduce children who squirm within the confines of adult decorum, as evidenced in many French mother-and-child portraits of the turn of the century. In Jacques-Louis David's rendering of his sister-in-law, Mme. Sériziat, of 7 1795, the affectedly natural posture of the sitter is quietly undermined by the genuinely natural restlessness and curiosity of her little boy, who seems to be fidgeting under the strain of the sittings and casting uneasy glances at his famous and infamous uncle, who had just been released from prison. This undercurrent of child liberation from the constraints of adulthood is no less emphatic, five years later, in a portrait of c.1800 by David's student, Antoine-Jean Gros, which depicts a certain Mme. 8

7 David, *Mme. Sériziat and her Son*, 1795   8 Gros, *Mme. Durand and her Daughter*, c.1800

9 Runge, *The Return of the Sons*, 1800–1801

Durand in a posture of classicizing elegance, while her young daughter seems almost to be attempting to wriggle out of the sedentary serenity imposed upon her mother.[6] This subcurrent of authentic childhood, whose rules appear more and more differentiated from those of adults, can be seen even more closely in the many paintings of lone children made in France in the later eighteenth century, from Chardin's, Greuze's, and Vigée-Lebrun's depictions of children engrossed in the construction of houses of cards or bored by the exertion of study to more confrontationally close-up images by David's student, Anne-Louis Girodet-Trioson, of the children in the artist's own foster family caught in moments of intense thought or reverie.[7]

It is against such a late eighteenth-century background that Runge's full-scale discovery of children, both as empirical realities and lofty symbols, must be measured. Throughout Runge's short but intense life—he was born in 1777 in Wolgast, near the Baltic Sea, and died of

10 Greuze, *The Village Bride*, 1761

consumption in Hamburg in 1810—the image of the family, whether his own or its allegorical reincarnations, loomed large. The emotional potency of his own family can already be seen in *The Return of the Sons*, a drawing of 1800–1801 that commemorates his and his eldest brother's return for a visit to the family home in Wolgast.[8] There, framed by the sheltering nature of the garden, the two of them are joyously and tearfully welcomed, left and center, by a chain of embracing parents and siblings. It is the kind of family scene already familiar in the work of Greuze, whose famous *Village Bride* of 1761 offers another lachrymose, closely knit community of parents and children, joyful yet sorrowing at the prospect of both losing a daughter and gaining a son and, it is hoped, grandchildren. Like Greuze, Runge here relegates the younger children to a literally inferior domain, a junior chorus whose emotional responses of grief, curiosity, and mindless innocence are to be observed on a level below the adult dramas enacted above.

15

11 Runge, *Parents with Child on Table*, 1800

But this generational hierarchy was equally susceptible to change, and perhaps nowhere more surprisingly than in another early drawing by Runge of 1800 that depicts an unidentified mother and father seated on opposite sides of a table upon which their infant is perched as a startling centerpiece.[9] So domestic a description, however, is immediately contradicted by the drawing style, which is clearly adapted from the chaste, classicizing outline engravings employed by John Flaxman to illustrate Homer, Aeschylus, Dante.[10] These publications, beginning in the 1790s, swept both their native England and the Continent, providing as it were the purest of blueprints for a new, unpolluted kind of image-making in which modeling and atmospheric effects were virtually annihilated in favor of the kind of planarity and incisive linear definition characteristic of Greek vases. Runge, like many of his

16

12 Flaxman, *Ulysses at the Table of Circe*, from *The Odyssey of Homer*, 1793

contemporaries—among them Blake, David, Ingres, even Goya—was stunned by Flaxman's primal simplicity,[11] and in the case of this family drawing may actually have found inspiration in one of Flaxman's illustrations to the *Odyssey* (1793) depicting Ulysses at the table of Circe.[12] But within Flaxman's rigorously abstract scheme of profiled figures and Greek furniture, Runge has permitted the most indecorous elements of domestic truth, from the father, resting with arm on table, to—most startlingly—the infant who, seated informally on the table top, demands eye-level attention from both its parents and the spectator.

    In terms of the history of art, this unexpectedly central focus upon the child, even within an adult world, brings to a climax the welling late eighteenth-century concern with childhood as a category of human development clearly to be distinguished from adulthood, not only in psychological and social terms but in medical ones as well; and it is surely worth mentioning that the progeny of Rousseau's innovating ideas on this subject could be found in later, German-speaking generations more closely contemporary to Runge himself. Not only was there the important educational reform practice and theory of the Swiss, Johann Heinrich Pestalozzi (1746–1827), but even closer to Runge in time and place, the work of a doctor, Christian August Struve (1767–1807), whose Hanover publication of 1798, *Über die Erziehung und Behandlung der Kinder in den ersten Lebensjaren; Ein Handbuch für alle Mütter, denen die Gesundheit ihrer Kinder am Herzen liegt* (On the Rearing and Treatment of Children in Their First Years of Life; a Handbook for all Mothers Who Care in Their Hearts for Their Children's Health), was successful enough to become a kind of Dr. Spock of the turn of the century, even prompting quickly an English translation (London, 1801–03).

Indeed, it was exactly in these years that Runge further magnified his concentration upon children alone, unaccompanied by their elders. In a drawing of 1799,[13] we stare solely at a pudgy infant, who totally dominates the drawing sheet, with his eyes fixed on the spectator and his ballooning cheeks almost seeming to exert pressure on the paper. And although the rest of the seated infant is only faintly drawn, it is possible to discern that with a prehensile grasp, characteristic of an infant, he holds a puppet in his left hand. And in another drawing of 1799,[14] this candid observation of real infant behaviour is further explored in a mixture of the abstract and the empirical so often found in Runge's work. Here the profile drawing of a baby, at first sight as idealized as a putto by Raphael, suddenly intrudes upon the facts of the nursery by noting the way the child firmly grasps his foot with his left hand so that he can in turn grasp the big toe with his right hand, a childhood commonplace (with perhaps classical resonances in the famous statue of Lo Spinario [the Thorn-Puller]) made even more true by the intense concentration registered on the infant's face.

Throughout his brief career, Runge's fresh excitement in focusing upon and recording these psychological and physiological facts of infants was balanced by a contradictory impulse to translate these

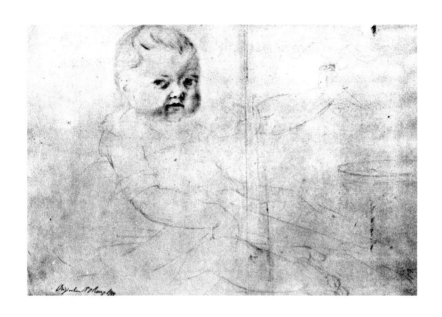

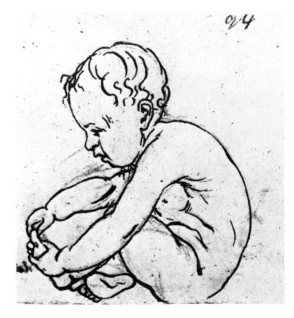

13 Runge, *Baby with Puppet*, 1799

14 Runge, *Seated Child Playing with his Toe*, 1799

15 Runge, *Mother at the Source*, 1804

marvelous data of the seen and felt world into a symbolic program. In a
15 lost painting of 1804, *Mother at the Source*,[15] what might have been
almost a rural maternity of a robust, peasantlike mother and child in a
secluded landscape takes on a mythical character, as the child, like
Narcissus, reaches with the most acutely observed outstretched hands for
its own watery reflection, echoing the actual narcissus that bows in
tandem at the right. Potentially only a rustic vignette, the image
reverberates in a symbolic realm of primordial character, in which the
universal motifs of mother, nature, water, mirror, self-discovery reach
backward to Christian and pagan mysticism as well as forward to
psychoanalytic territory. It is the kind of symbol-making that, in other
early works of Runge, would become far more explicit, as in his
illustrations to a printed edition of 1803 of *Minnelieder aus dem Schwäbische*

20

Zeitalter,[16] a modern translation of these medieval love songs by his friend Ludwig Tieck, who specialized in the nostalgic revival of fairy tales and folk legends. In a typical vignette,[17] we once again find an infant, related in its drawing style to the infant who holds his toe, but we have now moved to lofty symbolic domains, with an angel emerging from the rose blossom held by its stem in an infant's clenched grip and an allegorical lily of blossoming purity directed, like a heavenly trumpet blast, towards the name of Jehovah inscribed in a blaze of light. But again, this elevation of the child to Blake-like realms of heavenly, quasi-religious innocence, a creature as unpolluted as the ambient vision of nature, was constantly grounded by children scrutinized in a terrestrial world.

16

16 Runge, illustration to Tieck's *Minnelieder*, 1803

There are, for instance, indelibly candid drawings of a child and of an
adolescent seen in bed, at the beginning and end of a life cycle. As for the
17   end, there is a poignant, close-up image of Sophia Sieveking, the
nineteen-year-old daughter of a local merchant family, whom we are
obliged to observe at intimate range on what, in fact, was her deathbed.[18]
18   As for the beginning, there is an image of the angelic, but totally natural,
sleep of Runge's first child, Otto Sigismund, born on April 30, 1805. In
this lost drawing, probably of 1806,[19] the vantage point is disarmingly
real, that of an adult peering over an infant's crib the better to watch it
sleeping; and the detail of the two naked legs peeking out from under the
casually unstraightened blanket speaks even more emphatically of this
insistently authentic observation of a particular child, in this case the first
19   of the artist's four. Otto Sigismund looms still larger in a painting of
1805, the year of his birth,[20] a work probably sent to Runge's in-laws as
a Christmas present, together with a portrait of his wife Pauline, yet
another indication of the intense family dialogues that fused the artist's
life and work. Just as the most innovative Romantic painters tend to

break down a structural hierarchy centered on adults, forcing us to confront other living beings—animals, trees, flowers—on their own terms, so Runge, in this simple but amazingly potent canvas, makes us feel that perhaps for the first time in the history of art, we are actually face to face with a real baby. Here, Otto is seated upright in his highchair, dominating the cramped space so totally that we feel a confusion in scale, as if the chair were a huge throne (it is cropped on all sides) and the infant its regal master. Even more, Otto's baby flesh is thrust upon us with such exaggerated tactility that we immediately sense the compacted energies of a rapidly growing infant, from cheeks and neck folds down to the sausage-like hands and fingers that palpably affirm the table top. His physical growth, in fact, seems almost visible, with his chair hardly capable of restraining his bursting volumes and his dress (the costume now of a child and not, as it would have been in the earlier eighteenth century, of a miniature adult) almost becoming, even as we look at him, too tight for his arms. (The red of the dress, incidentally, may have its origins in Rousseau's idea that this was the favorite color of infants.)

17 OPPOSITE Runge,
*Sophie Sieveking on
her Deathbed*, 1810

18 Runge,
*Infant Sleeping
in Crib*, 1806

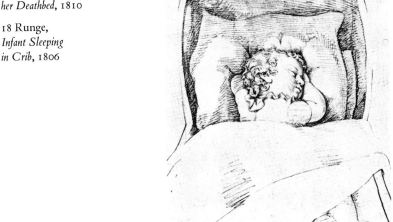

In the same year, 1805, Runge painted the portrait of another child, this time a commission from a friend in Hamburg, the bookseller Friedrich Perthes. In a preparatory drawing,[21] we first see the four-year-old Luise standing, as children do, on an adult's chair; and typically, the chair legs are cropped, forcing us into a maximum proximity with the mind and body of little Luise, who, instead of looking smaller than and therefore more remote from an adult world, somehow appears closer and more intense. This shift in scale, to that of a child's world, becomes even more acute in the finished painting (which irrelevantly, but unforgettably, once belonged to Adolf Hitler, who was presented with it on April 20, 1941).[22] The general idea of this portrait may well be derived from Dutch genre painting, and perhaps most particularly from Vermeer's *Girl Reading a Letter* in the Dresden Picture Gallery, where Runge could well have known it (and where it was first attributed, after its acquisition in 1742, to Rembrandt, and then de Hooch).[23] But Runge imposes upon this prosaic scene of a middle-class interior temporarily occupied by a single, preoccupied figure a different kind of magic from that found in Vermeer. Here, little Luise reigns mysteriously in an adult environment, dominating the chair and curtained window view by her firm posture—one pudgy hand grasping the chairback, the other her own neck—and, above all, by her moody, confrontational stare that would immerse us in her private, childlike reverie.[24] This uncanny loneliness is even further intensified by the distant view of specific Hamburg topography (the Lombard Bridge on the Alster and a no longer extant windmill),[25] a view that establishes a familiar Romantic polarity between near and far, enclosure and freedom that, in fact, will reach fruition in a far more famous painting, now securely dated 1822, of Caspar David Friedrich's own wife, Caroline, standing with her back to us before a window view of an outlet to the sea.[26]

Runge's treatment of light here also deserves comment, for the sun's rays are so intense on the blond hair and yellow dress of the little girl that she acquires a golden, almost supernatural glow, as if she both reflected and emanated this uncommonly powerful luminosity. Could there be here a kind of secular sanctification associated with the innocence of childhood? For at the same time, in 1805–06, Runge was working on

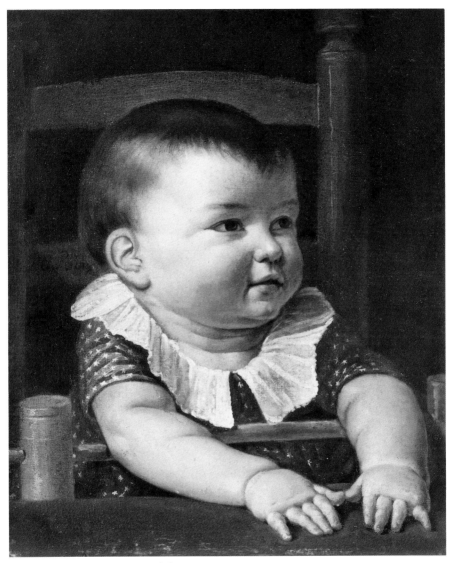

19 Runge, *Otto Sigismund in a Highchair*, 1805

20 Vermeer, *Girl Reading a Letter by the Window*, c.1655

21 BELOW LEFT Friedrich, *Woman at the Window*, 1822

22 BELOW Runge, preparatory drawing for *Luise Perthes*, 1805

23 OPPOSITE Runge, *Luise Perthes*, 1805

his far better known effort to revive moribund traditions of Christian
24 painting, *The Rest on the Flight into Egypt*.[27] Here, too, the Christ child,
created from the same pneumatic mold as Runge's infant son, Otto
Sigismund, seems to be both absorbing and emanating a mysterious
sunlight, whose source is invisible on the horizon, blocked from view by
the lightless Joseph and his ass, benighted symbols of the crumbling old
order. And we sense, too, the association of newness and purity with an
infant whose luminous contours, like that of the blossoming lily tree, are
at one with the power of sunlight to resurrect life and spirit. Tellingly,
Runge probably found inspiration here in another masterpiece from the
25 Dresden Picture Gallery, Correggio's *Nativity*, familiarly called *La
Notte* because of the nocturnal setting used as a natural contrast to the
supernatural luminosity of the Christ child in Mary's lap. Correggio's
miraculous vision, which Runge would have known not only in its
original version in Dresden but in a copy made by his friend Friedrich

28

24 OPPOSITE Runge,
*The Rest on the Flight
into Egypt*, 1805–06

25 Correggio, *Nativity*
("*La Notte*"), 1529–30

August von Klinkowström in 1805,[28] must have planted many seeds in Runge's own imaginative terrain, where he constantly sought equations between the natural and the supernatural and where he so often endowed children, like landscape, with a haloed radiance.

These organic mysteries, a kind of Romantic vitalism in which children are at one with the magical energies of sunlight and burgeoning landscape, are distilled most potently in Runge's most famous portrait of childhood, the record of the three children of his friend (and his brother Daniel's partner), the merchant Friedrich August Hülsenbeck, painted in 1805–06.[29] Although many precedents for this triple portrait have been suggested, most convincingly an unlocated painting of *c.* 1802 by Susanne Henry,[30] the Berlin-based daughter of the more famous artist Daniel Chodowiecki, nothing prepares us for this urgent and total immersion into the separate and private mysteries of a child's own domain. The two older children, Maria (born 1800) and August (born

27

29

26 Runge, preparatory drawing for *The Hülsenbeck Children*, 1805

1801), become surrogate parents, with the little girl (who resembles
23 Luise Perthes) looking and reaching back protectively toward her baby
brother Friedrich (born 1802) as she simultaneously steps forward in
tandem with the virile August, who holds a riding crop high above his
head. Both clasp the handle of the rustic baby carriage, dragging along
1   their infant sibling. Reigning over his own, much lower terrain, baby
Friedrich clutches the frame of his wooden carriage with one strong fist
and a sunflower stalk with the other, while his wide, unblinking stare

27 Runge, *The Hülsenbeck Children*, 1805–06

and swelling red cheeks exert a mesmerizing power and intensity echoed more heroically in his older brother August's vigorously self-assured expression and stance. As in the 1805 portraits of Luise Perthes and of Runge's own son (who, incidentally, wears the same red dress with its star pattern and white collar as baby Friedrich), we are thrust into a strange world scaled not to adults but to children. It is a point daringly amplified by the odd diminution in size of the white picket fence and the gabled house facade at the far right, against which the children, rather

23
19

than being dwarfed by adult carpentry and architecture, loom over us like rapidly growing giants. And these disconcerting shifts in scale, reflecting a child's perception of the adult world and previewing Alice in Wonderland's childlike disorientations to large and small, are further accentuated by the breathless back-and-forth rush from near to far, expanded by the distant view of Hamburg at the left and contracted in the picket fence's perspective thrust down the garden path at the right (at the far end of which, in a preparatory drawing, the most Lilliputian of figures, presumably the children's mother, stood waving from what appears to be a fantastically remote background).[31] Moreover, the light in this unexpectedly dreamlike garden, which now approaches the more familiar modern territory of illustrations to children's books, has an uncanny intensity explored in Runge's other works of 1805–06. In particular, the infant seems irradiated with a potent solar light that glows from the tips of his toes to his crown of blond hair, embodying a sense of irrepressible organic growth that then burgeons metaphorically toward the very top of the canvas in the heliotropic guise of a huge sunflower plant that he holds with the primitive strength of his infant hand. And extending this metaphor, the figures of his elder siblings, equally bathed in a generative sunlight, resemble two sturdy young trees, setting out with a rhymed step on the path of life.

29 Géricault, *Louise Vernet*, 1818–19

Although in any portrait gallery of Romantic children, the Hülsenbeck trio would be a hypnotic centerpiece, Runge's adventurous voyage into the mysterious world of a child's scale, psychology, and physiological closeness to the vital energies of nature was shared by other artists. In France, for instance, one can already find comparable explora‑ tions in the 1790s, as in a portrait of 1793 by Antoine‑Jean Gros of 28 Paulin des Hours Farel, [32] which, in scale, forces the spectator to move down to the eye‑level of the five‑year‑old boy who, like a primitive hunter, lurking far from his dwelling, has just bagged a goldfinch with his hat and now squeezes the squawking creature with evident triumph. This sense of direct contact with the rude physical and psychological forces of what appears a more primitive state of being is found, too, in many of Géricault's portraits of children, as in the unexpectedly enigmatic portrait of Horace Vernet's daughter Louise, painted about 29

33

28 Gros, *Paulin des Hours Farel*, 1793

1818, when she would have been three or four years old.[33] Seen without reference to an adult world, she seems, like Runge's children, to grow before our eyes, as does the uncannily huge cat she embraces in her lap. Both child and animal leave far behind eighteenth-century prototypes of adorable little girls and kittens cast in a Greuzian mold, plunging us instead into a dark, ominous world of ponderous giants, a child and a cat who, alone in a wild natural setting, refuse to conform to the polite rituals of adult domesticity.

Runge's fascination with real children, as well as allegorical infants, was once again fired by the birth of the second of his four children, Maria Dorothea, on June 25, 1807. In the following year, Runge explored a new psychological territory of childhood, the sibling relationship between Otto Sigismund, now three, and his new baby sister.[34] Again, we are obliged to confront head-on and close-up this infant couple, whose baby flesh dominates the small, unfinished canvas. Echoing Wordsworth's "The child is father of the man," Otto assumes the protective role of an adult, embracing his sister's shoulder and holding her left arm and clenched fist against his breast as she awkwardly reaches outward to grasp something with her right hand. Such proximity is even more disconcerting in the treatment of the eyes, for Otto fixes his gaze directly upon us while his baby sister displays the unfocused, strabismic stare often found in very young children. Runge's own words here enforce what the painting already shows us about Maria Dorothea, for in 1808, he had described her in a letter to his brother Daniel as "a totally charming child, so smooth and pudgy that it's a pleasure to see her, and so densely packed that bullets would bounce off her."[35]

How startlingly original this image of sibling love must have been in 1808–09 may be suggested by, among other earlier works of art, Germany's most famous sculpture of tender sisterhood, Johann Gottfried Schadow's marble of the Prussian princesses Louise and Frederica of Mecklenberg-Schwerin of 1795–97, an elegant classicizing fiction of unruffled sweetness and grace. Next to such emotional artifice, Runge's siblings have stormy passions, offering, as it were, the infant version of the artist's remarkable portrait of another family group that figured large in his life, *Wir Drei* (*We Three*) of 1805,[36] in which

34

30 Runge, *Otto Sigismund and Maria Dorothea*, 1808–09

Runge, his wife Pauline, and his brother Daniel seem to be exchanging an internal vow of love and trust that unites them not only through the clasping of hands and the embrace of shoulders but through deep emotions that seem to flow through their three bodies and souls. And again, although Runge's intensity in his exploration of these family relations may be unique, it nevertheless has many international counterparts, of which one of the most unexpected is a portrait by Benjamin West of his two sons, Raphael and Benjamin Jr., a painting of 1796 whose close-up depiction of fraternal intimacy against a dark, secluded landscape approaches the psychological drama Runge could reveal so hauntingly in his sibling duos and trios.[37]

32

31 Runge, *Wir Drei (We Three)*, 1805

32 West, *Raphael West and Benjamin West, Jr.*, 1796

33 OPPOSITE J. G. Schadow, *Princesses Louisa and Frederica*, 1795–97

For Runge, these mysterious family ties, already apparent in infants, could even conjure up more allegorical meditations on life cycles, on the ages of man, as implied in the full-length portrait of 1806 of the artist's 34 own parents, who stand rigidly in front of their home and next to a glimpse of the family shipping industry.[38] In contrast to this dour old couple, the very image of unsmiling middle-class property and propriety, are two of their grandchildren, Runge's own one-and-a-half-year-old son, Otto Sigismund, and the three-and-a-half-year-old Friedrich, the son of Runge's brother Jakob. The two young cousins seem to exist in a world parallel to, but remote from, that of their sternly inflexible grandparents. Echoing their ancestors' upright stance and clasped arms, the children nevertheless seem to be bathed in a natural vitality that has been extinguished in the dark, moribund domain of a much older generation. A brilliant sunlight not only illuminates but seems to nurture them, as it does the burgeoning plants and lilies that appear to be an integral part of the more unruly, natural world of childhood. Indeed, the two boys clasp and point to these blossoming flowers as if they were, in both body and spirit, a part of this natural kingdom so alien to the world of the grandparents, tightly constrained within the strict geometries of a diagonal walking stick and the flat, sharp-edged plane of their house. We sense here not only a generational continuity within the family, but a poignant contrast between childhood and old age, between a state of being that is mysteriously in tune with an irrepressible, primitive nature and one that has been repressed by the somber restrictions of civilization, a point underscored by the single rose, plucked and separated from its source in the earth and now used only as an adornment in the grandmother's hand.

Runge's visual definition of this vital, robust communion between children and nature, an elemental affinity that could quickly be translated into mystical, crypto-Christian symbols, pinpointed a major aspect of Romantic attitudes toward children, and left a powerful heritage of form and feeling both in his native Germany and elsewhere. It left its mark, for instance, in the occasional portrait drawings that the greatest German architect of Runge's generation, Karl Friedrich Schinkel, made of his own children. Looking at one of 1816 that depicts

34 Runge, *The Artist's Parents*, 1806

35 Schinkel, *Marie, the Artist's Daughter, at the Seashore*, 1816

36 Guérin, *Portrait of a Young Girl*, *c.*1800

his six-year-old daughter Marie at the seashore,[39] it is tempting to recall   35
the outmoded black-and-white contrast of Neoclassicism and Romanticism, for this once antagonistic polarity might be rejuvenated and
defended by a glimpse at another portrait of an artist's daughter painted
around 1800 by Pierre-Narcisse Guérin, working in the shadow of   36
David.[40] Next to the polished, artificial charm and grooming of the
French girl, Schinkel's daughter looks like an *enfant sauvage*. Liberated
by sand and sea as her blond hair streams in the wind, she reaches out
vigorously to gather, it would seem, the stones on the beach that are
faintly drawn in at the lower left. The spirit of Runge's natural child
is passionately alive here, from the almost feral stare to the forceful
thrust of her active arms. And again following Runge's footsteps into

37 Schinkel,
The Artist's Daughters,
Marie and Susanne, 1813

38 Wilhelm von Schadow,
The Artist's Children, 1830

uninhabited nature, Schinkel had earlier, in 1813, drawn a double
37   portrait of Marie (born September 2, 1810) and her younger sister,
Susanne (born November 23, 1811), in which the two tiny girls are
huddled together in a field of corn like two rabbits hiding in the
underbrush.[41] As in Runge's images of children, the scale here is topsy-
turvy, for the sisters loom so large in the dense compression of the
foreground that the cornfield behind them turns into an enormous jungle
that seems to extend far above the top edge.

Runge's disclosure of the awesome, elemental energies that fuse
children and landscape, however, was gently diluted by the next
generation of German painters, a point exemplified in another portrait of
38   an artist's children, those of Wilhelm von Schadow painted in 1830.
Here, the siblings, Sophie and Rudolf, still seem to echo many of
Runge's most intensely realized components, including the frontal
stares, the intimate communion between brother and sister, the secluded
landscape setting, and the hand that grasps wild flowers. Moreover, the
presence of a bare foot in water, of rabbits, of daisies and violets may be
translated as hidden Christian symbols, transforming, as was so often the

case in Runge, a secular scene into one fraught with sacred portent.[42] Nevertheless, it is equally apparent that by 1830, the harsh urgency of Runge's vision had been diffused in a formula more appropriate to the unruffled domesticity of a Biedermeier world. Indeed, in the case of Schadow's double portrait, we are tempted to discern the gentle inheritance of the painter's own father, Johann Gottfried Schadow, whose marble double portrait of the royal Prussian sisters continues to cast its artificial spell here in the polished, fluent contours and melting sweetness of expression that would accommodate children to the docile proprieties of mid-nineteenth-century family ideals.

33

As for Runge's ambitions to translate the freshly observed data of childhood and nature into grandly allegorical statements that swiftly and explicitly leave terrestrial reality for visionary climes, this, too, by the 1830s, was adapted into a more popularized, accessible form. For example, *Night*, one of Runge's preparatory drawings of 1803 for the projected four-part cycle of the *Tageszeiten* (*Times of Day*), was a particular favorite of the Romantic writer Clemens Brentano, who, in fact, owned a colored print of it and who would then use it as a basis for an illustration (by the Munich printmaker Kaspar Braun) for his classic German fairy tale, *Gockel, Hinkel, und Gackeleia*, first published in 1838.[43] Here, too, we feel a deflation of Runge's quest for the deepest verities, in which the mysterious hieroglyphs of airborne spirit children, in intimate communion with the cycles of nature, are transformed into appealing fantasies closer to Victorian Christmas decorations than to epic Romantic strivings to create icons for a new religion of nature and otherworldly innocence.

39

40

39 OPPOSITE Runge, *Night*, 1803

40 Brentano, illustration to *Gockel, Hinkel und Gackeleia*, 1838

41 Hodler, *The Chosen One*, 1893–94

Although in Germany Runge's passionate vision of childhood as fact and symbol was rapidly sweetened by mid-century, it was to be potently resurrected in many surprising ways by the end of the nineteenth century. In the case of the Swiss Symbolist, Ferdinand Hodler, Runge's odd mix of personal family history and transcendental goals is monumentally revived in the altar-like *Chosen One* of 1893–94, in which the artist's own six-year-old son Hector, presented in new-born nudity, in emblematic profile, and in prayerful posture, is placed beside a tiny, sanctified plot in which a sapling, clearly his botanical equivalent, has been planted. Above, six angels hover over the heights of a flowering mountain meadow in a celestial arc of embracing, protective symmetry.[44] It is an image that resonates back to Runge's own symbolic child, which, in its many variations, could so often resuscitate the iconic power of the infant Christ in a landscape of primal, sacred purity.

41

3

46

In the work of Hodler's exact contemporary, Vincent van Gogh, the more earthy, empirical side of Runge's observation of children was rejuvenated with an uncanny vigor that almost seems the immediate progeny of the German's family portraits. Although Hodler may well have been aware of Runge's art,[45] it is quite unlikely that Van Gogh could have known it. The affinities, however, are startling; and Van Gogh's portraits of baby Marcelle, the daughter born to the Arles postman Joseph Roulin and his wife Augustine on July 31, 1888, look like Runge's own babies reincarnate. Some three weeks after Marcelle was born, Van Gogh wrote to his sister Wil, "If I can get the mother and father to allow me to do a picture of it, I am going to paint a baby in a cradle one of these days."[46] It was a wish Runge had realized in 1806,   18 when he drew his own sleeping son in a crib, but in Van Gogh's case, this precise wish was not, in fact, fulfilled. What was painted was a series of fiercely intense close-up views of baby Marcelle in November-December 1888 that remarkably match and rival Runge's own awed perception of the bursting energy of growing infants. In a confrontational record of Marcelle's face,[47] saturated in a golden yellow that conveys the   42 kind of solar vitality with which Runge, too, had so often irradiated his

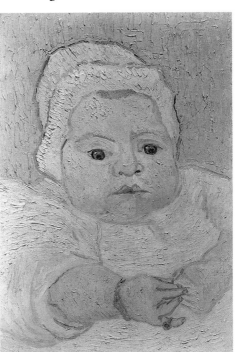

42 Van Gogh,
Marcelle Roulin, 1888

43 Van Gogh, *Mme. Roulin and her Baby*, 1888

44 OPPOSITE Runge, *The Artist's Wife and Son*, 1807

paintings of children, we are forced to stare at the coarse but urgent reality of an infant's pneumatic cheeks and clumsy grasp, here magni-

19 fied, as in the case of Runge's portrait of Otto Sigismund in a high chair, to dimensions that seem to push beyond the cramped confines of

43 the rectangular canvas. And in a portrait of the same baby, this time held by her mother, Van Gogh seems to revive Runge's 1807 portrait of his

44 wife Pauline holding the two-year-old Otto Sigismund.[48] In both, the child, like a tough young branch on a tree, seems the source of new life and energy, soon to overpower, one feels, the parental generation. Indeed, in the case of Van Gogh's portrait, Mme. Roulin is forced into a subsidiary role that completely defies the familar balance of mother and child, whether sacred or secular, in Western painting, a balance that Van Gogh had, in fact, elected to maintain in a more conventional portrait of Mme. Roulin and her baby executed shortly afterwards.[49]

48

45 Renoir, *Studies of the Berard Children*, 1881

Once more enshrined, so to speak, by the golden yellow background, baby Marcelle contradicts, too, the more familiar sanctifications of childhood in the work of Van Gogh's French contemporaries. A glimpse at almost any example of Renoir's countless portraits of childhood will enforce this point. In his 1881 portrait of the four 45 children of the banker Paul Berard, ranging in age from one to thirteen, Renoir presents a bouquet of adorable vignettes, a secular chorus of disembodied angels.[50] Whether sleeping infants or alert little girls and boys, they are sanctified in quite a different way from Van Gogh's and Runge's children, conforming to Rococo and Victorian fantasies of children as cuddly innocents of cotton-candy sweetness and softness rather than as mysterious vessels of primitive energy through which nature's most awesome secrets could be intuited. Within Renoir's 42 cherubic domain, Van Gogh's vision of baby Marcelle would be the

50

harshest of intruders, an ungainly mass of infant flesh struggling to grow and to blossom, like the toughest sunflower stalk pushing relentlessly upward for its vital nourishment.

Such a vision of children as tough, animal beings, deeply rooted in nature, was perpetuated in Runge's own country, especially in the milieu of German art of the 1920s, by which time the artist had become, with Caspar David Friedrich, a father figure in the growingly nationalist view of Germany's cultural past. Runge's ghost—art-historically resurrected in an article of 1923 by Paul Friedrich Schmidt on Runge's relevance for modern German art[51]—reappears in the style known as "Neue Sachlichkeit" (traditionally, if not too precisely, translated as "New Objectivity"), a style in which the literal and metaphorical ruins of post-war Germany are reconstructed with such enduring clarity and firmness that the resulting images often have an eerie, robotic quality. For masters like Otto Dix and Georg Schrimpf,[52] Runge's children, with   46

46 Dix, *Nelly in the Flowers*, 1924

47 Sander, *Peasant Children, Westerwald*, 1923

their indomitable sense of pressing physical reality, provided the strongest foundations for many of their own depictions of the infants who were born in the ashes of the war. Among such allusions, no homage to Runge is as direct and forceful as Dix's portrait of his own daughter, Nelly.[53] Born in 1923, the infant was painted by her father only months later, in 1924, prompting what might also be considered an addition to Runge's *Hülsenbeck Children* of the fourth and youngest member of the nursery. Like baby Friedrich, Nelly holds one of the wild flowers that surround and tower over her like a jungle, symbolically uniting her with this burgeoning underbrush. Her cheeks and arms almost visibly swelling before our eyes, Nelly is herself a force of nature. The long-lived sentimental equation of tender children and delicate flowers is assaulted here, as in Runge, by a fusion of human and botanical energies that evoke the stuff of Darwinian survival. 46

27

And even in the realm of German photography of the 1920s, Runge, and particularly the *Hülsenbeck Children*, seem to live again in the work of August Sander. Among his documentary photos of a vast sociological spectrum of post-war citizens of the Weimar Republic, ranging from unskilled workers to the intellectual elite, a group of peasant children from the Westerwald, not far from Sander's own home in Cologne, presents the most uningratiating image of childhood that, in its glowering frontality and relentless sense of animal will to live and to perpetuate the species, translates Runge's awe before the child as a natural vehicle of brute vitality into the grim facts of simple biological survival in the devastation of post-war Germany. 47

But in our century, Runge's images of childhood long outlived their immediate relevance to his own nation in the 1920s. After 1945, his fame so increased that by now, when his paintings have traveled outside German borders to London, Paris, and New York, and when his major works are reproduced in all international surveys of Romantic art, the archetypal Runge child in its mysterious manmade or natural environment could be recreated in the universal language of childhood fantasy, the illustrated fairy tale, a territory Runge himself had begun to explore in his illustrations to Tieck's *Minnelieder* and that Brentano would share in his Runge-inspired illustration to *Gockel, Hinkel, und* 16

40

Gackeleia. It is perhaps no surprise, then, that one of the most renowned twentieth-century creators of children's books, Maurice Sendak, began in the late 1970s to immerse himself in the magic domain of Runge's drawings and paintings, finding there, and in other German Romantic art, nostalgic and often obsessive inspiration for many of the enchanted settings and brooding dramatis personae of his own publications of the 1980s. Most prominent among Sendak's empathic excursions into Runge's mythic realm are those found in *Outside Over There* (1981), in which we feel that we have fallen through a magic looking-glass into an anthology of paintings and drawings by Runge and his contemporaries and watched them all quicken. A Pygmalion to Runge's Galatea, Sendak seems to have loved and worshiped the Hülsenbeck children so much that he can make them and their garden spring to life before our eyes. In the half-title illustration to *Outside Over There* we see Ida and her infant brother, a pair of awkwardly tender siblings who look like modern reincarnations of the Hülsenbeck children, walking past that unforgettable picket fence and burst of sunflowers once found in a garden outside Hamburg in 1805.

48

27

48 Sendak, half-title illustration from *Outside Over There*, 1981

49 Sendak, "So the goblins came. They pushed their way in and pulled baby out, leaving another all made of ice," from *Outside Over There*, 1981

In another, more complex illustration to the same book, Sendak offers an even wider range of allusions to Runge and his contemporaries. The low-ceilinged interior, more suited to the scale of children than to that of adults, is adapted, especially in the treatment of the window, from a frequently reproduced portrait by Georg Friedrich Kersting of Caspar David Friedrich in his lonely studio;[54] and Ida, now playing the German Romantic *Wunderhorn*, made famous in Brentano and Achim

49

Arnim's collection of folksongs, *Des Knaben Wunderhorn* (The Boy's Magic Horn), stands before another window invaded by the most vital growth of sunflowers, as if she were a descendant not only of the Hülsenbeck children but even of Luise Perthes. And her infant brother, now transformed into an ice baby by the demonic goblins already lurking in the title page, is an even more horrific transformation of baby Friedrich Hülsenbeck, borrowed not so much from Runge's completed painting as from the preparatory outline drawing, in which the infant's wide-eyed stare appears more mysteriously blank and frozen. Lastly, cropped in the upper righthand corner, there is a framed and painted image of parental authority, a face that firmly but stealthily reigns over this magical world of looming children and their fears and joys. Although generic as a German Romantic self-portrait, perhaps this presiding genius is the ghost of Philipp Otto Runge as he depicted himself in 1810, at the very end of his short life, a ghost that continues to haunt not only artists but the rest of us with the progeny of his Romantic children.[55]

23

26

50

50 Runge, *Self-Portrait in Brown Cloak*, 1809–10

NOTES

1 On this lost drawing, see the essential monograph and catalogue raisonné: Jörg Traeger, *Philipp Otto Runge und sein Werk*, Munich, 1975, no. 392. Traeger's monumental study was amplified to a more international scope in a major exhibition catalogue: Werner Hofmann, ed., *Runge in seiner Zeit*, Hamburg, Kunsthalle (pub. Munich), 1977. Both works are now indispensable tools of modern research.

2 The modern classics in this field are Philippe Ariès, *L'Enfant et la vie familiale sous l'Ancien Régime*, Paris, 1960; and Lawrence Stone, *The Family, Sex and Marriage in England, 1500–1800*, London and New York, 1977.

3 This theme is fully treated in Carol Duncan, "Happy Mothers and Other New Ideas in French Art," *Art Bulletin*, LV, December 1973, pp. 570–83.

4 An earlier sketch appeared at the 1765 Salon, but the final version, though listed in the 1769 Salon catalogue, was apparently not exhibited. See Edgar Munhall, *Jean-Baptiste Greuze, 1725–1805*, Hartford, Wadsworth Atheneum, 1976, no. 46.

5 For a detailed account of Graff's portrait, see Franz Zelger, *Stiftung Oskar Reinhart Winterthur*, I, Zurich, 1977, no. 85. Among many other examples of this new intimacy in late eighteenth-century artists' portraits of their own families, John Singleton Copley's (1776–77) is conspicuous (Washington, National Gallery).

6 On Gros's portrait, see *Gros, ses amis, ses élèves*, Paris, Petit Palais, 1936, no. 21.

7 Girodet's portraits of children are surely the most symptomatic of this trend in France. They are discussed most fully in George Levitine, *Girodet-Trioson: An Iconographical Study*, New York and London, 1978, pp. 322–30.

8 For a fuller account of this family scene, see Traeger, *op. cit.*, no. 120

9 *Ibid.*, no. 147.

10 For an early discussion of Flaxman and his impact on art around 1800, see my doctoral thesis, *The International Style of 1800; A Study in Linear Abstraction*, New York University, 1956, reprinted New York and London, 1976, pp. 114 ff.

11 On this, see Peter-Klaus Schuster, "Runge und Flaxman," in *Runge in seiner Zeit, op. cit.*, p. 262.

12 This is Plate 16 in the original London edition of 1793.

13 Traeger, *op. cit.*, no. 43.

14 *Ibid.*, no. 73.

15 *Ibid.*, no. 298.

16 On this edition, see *ibid.*, nos. 259–64. For a full account of relations between artist and writer, see J. B. C. Grundy, *Runge and Tieck*, Strasbourg, 1930.

17 Traeger, *op. cit.*, no. 262A.

18 The drawing is related to a lost painting. See *ibid.*, nos. 529–30.

19 *Ibid.*, no. 356.

20 *Ibid.*, no. 313.

21 *Ibid.*, no. 308.

22 *Ibid.*, no. 310.

23 See *The Complete Paintings of Vermeer* (catalogue by Piero Bianconi), New York, 1977, no. 8, for these attributions. The catalogue entry here gives 1754 as the

date of the painting's acquisition in Paris, but the Dresden catalogues give 1742.

24 Runge's painting is clearly an archetypal example of the Romantic motif of the open window, discussed most fully in Lorenz Eitner's classic study, "The Open Window and the Storm-Tossed Boat: An Essay in the Iconography of Romanticism," *Art Bulletin*, XXXVII, December 1955, pp. 281–90. Eitner's examples date from *c.* 1810 ff., and omit Runge's portrait, whose date, 1805, would give it a remarkable precocity in this development.

25 Runge, in fact, made a very detailed drawing of this Hamburg view. See Traeger, *op. cit.*, no. 309.

26 This connection, and many others, between the two greatest painters of German Romanticism is suggested in Jörg Traeger, "Philipp Otto Runge und Caspar David Friedrich," in *Runge: Fragen und Antworten; Ein Symposium der Hamburger Kunsthalle*, Munich, 1979, pp. 96–114.

27 The classic study of this painting and its symbolism of light and landscape is found in Otto von Simson, "Philipp Otto Runge and the Mythology of Landscape," *Art Bulletin*, XXIV, December 1942, pp. 335–50. See also Traeger, *op. cit.*, no. 322.

28 On Klinkowström, see *ibid.*, p. 18.

29 *Ibid.*, no. 312.

30 See Christian Adolf Isermeyer, *Philipp Otto Runge*, Berlin, 1940, p. 115; and *Runge in seiner Zeit, op. cit.*, p. 232.

31 For more on this preparatory drawing, see Traeger, *op. cit.*, no. 311.

32 On Gros's portrait, see *Gros, ses amis, ses élèves, op. cit.*, no. 10.

33 The same dark, rebellious mood is apparent in three other amazing child portraits by Géricault: Olivier Bro, astride an unusually ferocious dog; Alfred Dedreux, in a Byronic pose in wild nature; and Alfred and Elizabeth Dedreux, in a brooding sibling colloquy. On these and the Louise Vernet portrait, see Philippe Grunchec, ed., *Tout l'oeuvre peint de Géricault*, Paris, 1978, nos. 136, 95, 116, 135.

34 Traeger, *op. cit.*, no. 433.

35 Karl Friedrich Degner, ed., *Philipp Otto Runge; Briefe in der Urfassung*, Berlin, 1940, pp. 346–48.

36 Traeger, *op. cit.*, no. 306.

37 On this exceptional West portrait, see Helmut von Erffa and Allen Staley, *The Paintings of Benjamin West*, New Haven and London, 1986, no. 543.

38 Traeger, *op. cit.*, no. 355. I have discussed the painting before in some detail in my *Modern Painting and the Northern Romantic Tradition*, London and New York, 1975, pp. 50–51.

39 For the most recent information about this drawing, see *La peinture allemande à l'époque du Romantisme*, Paris, Orangerie des Tuileries, 1976–77, no. 225.

40 This, at least, is the traditional identification of the young sitter. See Boulogne-sur-Mer, Musée des Beaux-Arts et d'Archéologie, *Catalogue; Guide Illustré*, 1926, p. 6.

41 On this drawing, see Carl von Lorck, *Karl Friedrich Schinkel*, Berlin, 1939, p. 27.

42 For an account of the veiled Christian symbolism in Schadow's double portrait, see *German Masters of the Nineteenth Century*, New York, The Metropolitan Museum of Art, 1981, no. 75.

43 I already indicated this visual borrowing in *Modern Painting . . . , op. cit.*, p. 65. For more on Brentano's enthusiasm for Runge and his particular knowledge of *Night*, see Traeger, *op. cit.*, pp. 178, 188.

44 For more on Hodler's affinities with Runge, see Rosenblum, *Modern Painting . . . , op. cit.*, pp. 122–26.

45 That Runge was known in German-speaking circles of the later nineteenth century is evident from the fact that Richard Muther devoted some nine pages to him in his epic *Geschichte der Malerei im 19. Jahrhundert*, II, Munich, 1893, pp. 1–9.

46 Quoted in Ronald Pickvance, *Van Gogh in Arles*, New York, 1984, p. 223.

47 There are two other close copies of this portrait by Van Gogh (F 441, 442).

48 Traeger, *op. cit.*, no. 374. I have already suggested this comparison in *Modern*

Painting . . ., *op. cit.*, pp. 87–88, as well as other affinities between Van Gogh and Runge.

49 See Pickvance, *op. cit.*, p. 228.

50 On the Berard portrait, see *Renoir*, London, Hayward Gallery, 1985, no. 60.

51 "Runge und die Gegenwart," *Der Cicerone*, xv, 1923, pp. 457–64. On Runge and "Die neue Sachlichkeit," see also Traeger, *op. cit.*, p. 198.

52 Richard Morphet, of the Tate Gallery, kindly called my attention to Schrimpf's *Drei Kinder (Three Children)*, a painting of 1926 that seems a direct paraphrase of the *Hülsenbeck Children*. (Illustrated in Wolfgang Storch, *Georg Schrimpf und Maria Uhden, Leben und Werk*, Berlin, 1985, p. 145.)

53 On *Nelly*, see Fritz Löffler, *Otto Dix, Leben und Werk*, Vienna and Munich, 1967, p. 60. For a remarkably vivid and unusually early account of *Nelly*, see Alfred H. Barr, Jr., "Otto Dix," an article first written in 1929 and printed two years later in *The Arts*, xvii, January 1931, pp. 234–51, now reprinted in Irving Sandler and Amy Newman, eds., *Defining Modern Art; Selected Writings of Alfred H. Barr, Jr.*, New York, 1986, pp. 147–53. In Barr's words, which might well refer to Runge's children, "The pudgy hands, the inflated cheeks and staring eyes, the top heavy head, the puppet-like intentness, those strange inhuman qualities of babies are remarkably expressed."

54 This painting of 1812 is conveniently reproduced in, among other places, William Vaughan's excellent survey, *German Romantic Painting*, New Haven and London, 1980, p. 67.

55 Topically, Sendak is publishing this year (1988) an edition of Grimm's fairy tales with illustrations that continue to recreate a widening range of Runge's imagery.

LIST OF ILLUSTRATIONS

Measurements are given in centimetres, followed by inches in brackets.

Height precedes width.

1 PHILIPP OTTO RUNGE
Detail of *The Hülsenbeck Children*
See Ill. 27

2 LEONARDO DA VINCI
*Vitruvian Man, c.*1490
Drawing, 34.3 × 24.5 $(13\frac{1}{2} \times 9\frac{5}{8})$
Accademia, Venice
Photo Soprintendenza alle Gallerie, Venice

3 RUNGE
The Child, 1809
Drawing, 15 × 20.5 $(5\frac{7}{8} \times 8\frac{1}{8})$
Whereabouts unknown

4 JEAN-BAPTISTE GREUZE
*La Mère Bien-Aimée, c.*1769
Oil on canvas, 99 × 131 $(39 \times 51\frac{5}{8})$
Private collection

5 SIR JOSHUA REYNOLDS
Lady Cockburn and her Children, 1773
Oil on canvas, 141.6 × 113 $(55\frac{3}{4} \times 44\frac{1}{2})$
National Gallery, London

6 ANTON GRAFF
*The Artist's Family with the portrait of Johann
    G. Sulzer,* 1785
Oil on canvas, 196 × 148 $(77\frac{1}{8} \times 58\frac{1}{4})$
Museum Stiftung Oskar Reinhart,
    Winterthur, Switzerland

7 JACQUES-LOUIS DAVID
Madame Sériziat and her Son, 1795
Oil on canvas, 131 × 96 $(51\frac{5}{8} \times 38\frac{3}{4})$
Photo Lauros-Giraudon

8 ANTOINE-JEAN GROS
*Madame Durand and her Daughter, c.*1800
Oil on canvas, 97 × 75 $(38\frac{1}{8} \times 29\frac{1}{2})$
Private collection
Photo Giraudon

9 RUNGE
The Return of the Sons, 1800–1801
Drawing, 44.7 × 65 $(17\frac{5}{8} \times 25\frac{5}{8})$
Kupferstichkabinett, Kunsthalle, Hamburg
Photo Kleinhempel

10 JEAN-BAPTISTE GREUZE
The Village Bride, 1761
Oil on canvas, 92 × 117 $(36\frac{1}{4} \times 46)$
Louvre, Paris
Photo Giraudon

11 RUNGE
Parents with Child on Table, 1800
Drawing, 21 × 55 $(8\frac{1}{4} \times 21\frac{5}{8})$
Kupferstichkabinett, Kunsthalle, Hamburg
Photo Kleinhempel

12 JOHN FLAXMAN
Ulysses at the Table of Circe
Plate 16 from *The Odyssey of Homer,*
    London, 1793
Engraving, 17.2 × 24.5 $(6\frac{3}{8} \times 9\frac{5}{8})$

13 RUNGE
Baby with Puppet, 1799
Drawing, 40 × 58.4 $(15\frac{3}{4} \times 23)$
Private collection

14 RUNGE
Seated Child playing with his Toe, 1799
Drawing
Dimensions and whereabouts unknown

15 RUNGE
Mother at the Source, 1804
Oil on canvas, 62.5 × 78.1 ($24\frac{5}{8}$ × $30\frac{3}{4}$)
Formerly Kunsthalle, Hamburg. Destroyed
  by fire in 1931

16 RUNGE
Illustration to J. L. Tieck, *Minnelieder aus dem
  Schwäbischen Zeitalter neu Bearbeitet und
  Herausgegeben*, Berlin, 1803
Engraving, 10 × 8 (4 × $3\frac{1}{8}$)

17 RUNGE
Sophia Sieveking on her Deathbed, 1810
Drawing, 43.4 × 50.8 ($17\frac{1}{8}$ × 20)
Kupferstichkabinett, Kunsthalle, Hamburg
Photo Kleinhempel

18 RUNGE
Infant Sleeping in Crib, 1806
Drawing, 28.3 × 24.3 ($11\frac{1}{8}$ × $9\frac{5}{8}$)
Whereabouts unknown

19 RUNGE
Otto Sigismund in a Highchair, 1805
Oil on canvas, 40 × 55.5 ($15\frac{3}{4}$ × $21\frac{7}{8}$)
Kunsthalle, Hamburg
Photo Kleinhempel

20 JAN VERMEER
Girl Reading a Letter by the Window, c. 1655
Oil on canvas, 83 × 64.5 ($32\frac{5}{8}$ × $25\frac{3}{8}$)
Gemäldegalerie Alte Meister, Staatliche
  Kunstsammlungen, Dresden

21 CASPAR DAVID FRIEDRICH
Woman at the Window, 1822
Oil on canvas, 44 × 37 ($17\frac{3}{8}$ × $14\frac{5}{8}$)
Staatliche Museen Preussischer Kulturbesitz,
  Nationalgalerie, Berlin (West)
Photo Jörg P. Anders

22 RUNGE
Luise Perthes, 1805
Drawing, 60.2 × 45.2 ($23\frac{3}{4}$ × $17\frac{3}{4}$)
Sammlung der Zeichnungen, Staatliche
  Museen, Berlin, DDR

23 RUNGE
Luise Perthes, 1805
Oil on canvas, 143.5 × 95 ($56\frac{1}{2}$ × $37\frac{3}{8}$)
Staatliche Kunstsammlungen, Weimar
Photo Roland Drossler

24 RUNGE
The Rest on the Flight into Egypt, 1805–06
Oil on canvas, 96.5 × 129.5 (38 × 51)
Kunsthalle, Hamburg
Photo Kleinhempel

25 CORREGGIO
Nativity ("La Notte"), 1529–30
Oil on canvas, 256.5 × 188 (101 × 74)
Gemäldegalerie Alte Meister, Staatliche
  Kunstsammlungen, Dresden

26 RUNGE
The Hülsenbeck Children, 1805
Drawing, 55.1 × 61 ($21\frac{3}{4}$ × 24)
Kupferstichkabinett, Kunsthalle, Hamburg
Photo Kleinhempel

27 RUNGE
The Hülsenbeck Children, 1805–06
Oil on canvas, 131.5 × 143.5 ($51\frac{3}{4}$ × $56\frac{1}{2}$)
Kunsthalle, Hamburg

28 ANTOINE-JEAN GROS
Paulin des Hours Farel, 1793
Oil on canvas, 76 × 98 ($29\frac{7}{8}$ × $38\frac{5}{8}$)
Musée des Beaux-Arts, Rennes
Photo Giraudon

29 THÉODORE GÉRICAULT
Louise Vernet, 1818–19
Oil on canvas, 60.5 × 50.5 ($23\frac{7}{8}$ × $19\frac{7}{8}$)
Louvre, Paris
Photo Réunion des Musées Nationaux

30 RUNGE
Otto Sigismund and Maria Dorothea, 1808–09
Oil on canvas, 38.5 × 49.5 ($15\frac{1}{8}$ × $19\frac{1}{2}$)
Kunsthalle, Hamburg
Photo Kleinhempel

31 RUNGE
Wir Drei (We Three), 1805
Oil on canvas, 100 × 122 ($39\frac{3}{8}$ × 48)
Formerly Kunsthalle, Hamburg. Destroyed
by fire in 1931
Photo Kunsthalle, Hamburg

32 BENJAMIN WEST
Raphael West and Benjamin West, Jr., 1796
Oil on canvas, 89.5 × 71.7 ($35\frac{1}{4}$ × $28\frac{1}{4}$)
Nelson-Atkins Museum of Art, Kansas
City, Missouri (Nelson Fund)

33 JOHANN GOTTFRIED SCHADOW
Princesses Louisa and Frederica, 1795–97
Marble, H.172 ($67\frac{3}{4}$)
Nationalgalerie, Staatliche Museen, Berlin,
DDR

34 RUNGE
The Artist's Parents, 1806
Oil on canvas, 196 × 131 ($77\frac{1}{8}$ × $51\frac{1}{2}$)
Kunsthalle, Hamburg

35 KARL FRIEDRICH SCHINKEL
Marie, the Artist's Daughter, at the Seashore,
1816
Drawing, 53.5 × 42.4 (21 × $16\frac{3}{4}$)
Sammlung der Zeichnungen, Staatliche
Museen, Berlin, DDR

36 PIERRE-NARCISSE GUÉRIN
Portrait of a Young Girl, c.1800
Oil on canvas, 46 × 38 ($18\frac{1}{8}$ × 15)
Musée des Beaux-Arts, Boulogne-sur-Mer
Photo Réunions des Musées Nationaux

37 KARL FRIEDRICH SCHINKEL
The Artist's Daughters, Marie and Susanne,
1813

Drawing
Formerly Nationalgalerie, Berlin. Lost

38 WILHELM VON SCHADOW
The Artist's Children, 1830
Oil on canvas, 138 × 110 ($54\frac{3}{8}$ × $43\frac{1}{4}$)
Kunstmuseum, Düsseldorf

39 RUNGE
Night, 1803
Drawing, 44.1 × 51.7 ($17\frac{3}{8}$ × $20\frac{3}{8}$)
Kunsthalle, Hamburg

40 KASPAR BRAUN after CLEMENS
BRENTANO
Illustration to *Gockel, Hinkel und Gackeleia*,
1838
Lithograph, 18.5 × 11.5 ($7\frac{1}{4}$ × $4\frac{1}{2}$)

41 FERDINAND HODLER
The Chosen One, 1893–94
Tempera and oil on canvas, 219 × 296
($86\frac{1}{4}$ × $116\frac{1}{2}$)
Gottfried Keller Stiftung, Kunstmuseum,
Bern

42 VINCENT VAN GOGH
Marcelle Roulin, 1888
Oil on canvas, 35 × 23.9 ($13\frac{3}{4}$ × $9\frac{3}{8}$)
National Gallery of Art, Washington,
D.C., Chester Dale Collection 1962

43 VINCENT VAN GOGH
Madame Roulin and her Baby, 1888
Oil on canvas, 63.5 × 51 (25 × 20)
The Metropolitan Museum of Art, New
York, Robert Lehman Collection, 1975
[1975.1.231]

44 RUNGE
The Artist's Wife and Son, 1807
Oil on canvas, 96.5 × 72.5 (38 × $28\frac{1}{2}$)
Staatliche Museen Preussischer Kulturbesitz,
Nationalgalerie, Berlin (West)
Photo Jörg P. Anders

45 PIERRE-AUGUSTE RENOIR
Studies of the Berard Children, 1881
Oil on canvas, 62.6 × 82 ($24\frac{5}{8} \times 32\frac{1}{4}$)
Sterling and Francine Clark Art Institute,
  Williamstown, Massachusetts

46 OTTO DIX
Nelly in the Flowers, 1924
Oil on canvas, 81 × 55.5 ($31\frac{7}{8} \times 21\frac{7}{8}$)
Private collection

47 AUGUST SANDER
Peasant Children, Westerwald, 1923
Photograph
From Gunther Sander, *August Sander—
  Menschen ohne Masken*, published by
  Verlag C. J. Bucher, Lucerne and
  Frankfurt, 1971 (*August Sander,
  Photographer Extraordinary*, Thames and
  Hudson, London, 1973)

48 MAURICE SENDAK
Half-title illustration from *Outside Over
  There*, published by Harper and Row,
  New York, and The Bodley Head,
  London, 1981. Copyright Maurice
  Sendak
10.6 × 15.8 ($4\frac{3}{16} \times 6\frac{1}{4}$)

49 MAURICE SENDAK
Illustration to *Outside Over There*, published
  by Harper and Row, New York, and
  The Bodley Head, London, 1981.
  Copyright Maurice Sendak
22.8 × 25.2 ($9 \times 9\frac{15}{16}$)

50 RUNGE
Self-Portrait in Brown Cloak, 1809–10
Oil on panel, 48 × 47 ($18\frac{7}{8} \times 18\frac{1}{2}$)
Kunsthalle, Hamburg
Photo Kleinhempel